TIME.

MONEY.

STATUS.

RELATIONSHIPS.

PEACE OF MIND.

Alla Adam

Copyright © 2024 Alla Adam

The author's moral rights have been asserted.

All rights reserved.

Sharing is caring, but stealing is a no-go zone.

Remember to mention the author's name if you use a quotation from this book. And, if you want to tap into the goldmine of insights within these pages, reach out to the author via

https://www.allaadam.com/

Let's respect each other and make progress happen together.

PREFACE

Alla Adam is the author of three Playbooks:

Million Dollar Coach Playbook

Million Dollar Investor Playbook

Million Dollar Negotiator Playbook

and

TAM Journal

DEDICATION

To G.B., who is the best source of inspiration. Ever.

CONTENTS

Foreword

Instructions for use

Time.	1
Money.	8
Status.	24
Relationships.	36
Peace of mind.	44
Final notes	51
Big and special thanks	53
The very final note	54
Appendix 1 MDCP	56
Appendix 2 MDIP	61
Appendix 3 MDNP	65

Appendix 4 TAM   70

Appendix 5 TAC   74

Appendix 6 MLSW   76

Appendix 7 NPW   81

Appendix 8 SHW   83

Appendix 9 SPPW   86

About the author

FOREWORD

You are about to see what happens when a Book and a Playbook have a baby. Inside, you will find everything you wanted to say but couldn't find the right words. Also, it is your shortest foreword ever.

INSTRUCTIONS FOR USE

Why you should read T.M.S.R.P.

This book is for anyone who has to deal with life every day. Whether you are a startup founder, a venture capitalist, a top manager of a multibillion-dollar company, a teacher, a pilot, or a coach, you will be confronted by the same questions time and time again: How do I better time my day, year, and life? How do I confidently money-make my way to financial freedom? How do I assertively status-up my career? How do I relationship better? How do I train myself to mind peace of mind?

What you will find inside T.M.S.R.P.

Three hundred sixty-five [one for each day of the year] well-known and not-so-well-known pieces of wisdom that will help you live life better and be unapologetically happy on your terms. Don't expect straight answers. Be prepared to be challenged. Expect food for thought and action. You'll acquire the kind of knowledge with which you can transform your life and impress your loved ones, friends, colleagues, and partners.

How to use T.M.S.R.P.

This isn't just a book; it's a guide designed to be accessible on your phone, tablet, computer, or table around the clock. You can copy out the pieces that resonate most with you, work with them, develop and improve them, and make them your own. It doesn't matter at what page you start—it works bottom up and top down. Whether you're gearing up for a TED talk, a pitch competition, a tough conversation, an annual performance review, whether a difficult decision lies ahead of you or an exhausting negotiation behind you, whether you're reassessing your business strategy, investment plans, personal or professional relationships, or just want to get to know yourself better—T.M.S.R.P. is your reliable guide.

TIME.

***

Time is red because it is immediate. Significant. Dynamic. Vital like the sun. Its impact on your life is inevitable.

***

Time is red and urgent, like an alarm, a stop sign, a Netflix logo, the most common rose flower, and a Red Delicious apple.

***

Building a life worth living requires time. Time requires money. Money requires attention. Attention requires you. Unless you are a random trust fund baby, there's no other way around it.

***

Growth is not a strategy—it is a tactic. And tactics require time.

***

Make investments as you go through life. As you move through your day, keep a sharp eye out for investment ideas. Train yourself to look at everything as a potential investment material. Create a log of your investment ideas. Then, give yourself more details—research at least one idea from it per day. Give each idea a gestation time depending on the level of risk it involves. Then, make a decision – invest or not invest. Don't give yourself any other options. Time is used best when it's used often and for good reasons.

***

You can choose to find your voice now or continue to ignore it.

***

Here's a killer productivity tip—sit down and do it.

***

You don't need more time. You need more focus. And then you need to decide.

***

Your life is not a job. A job is not your life. Your time is both your life and your job.

***

The mindset of a VC fund is simple: Can this company return the fund? Deploy it to test your idea/project towards the potential to return the fund: Can my idea/project return the fund? This simple mind tweak is the best time saver.

***

Even if the idea is big, the time is right, and the resources are available, someone other than you might be the right person to do it. Accept it and move on.

***

First, figure out what you're good at without trying. Then try.

***

You'll be most successful where you're most intensely interested. Don't invest your time in what you are not interested in.

***

Exponential growth occurs when change happens at an accelerating rate rather than a constant one. Not many things can accelerate change, but this is how you save time.

***

Positive judgment is the art of knowing what to ignore.

***

The DDD Rule always works: Deadlines Drive Decisions.

***

Realistic expectations don't lead to stress and time abuse.

***

If you notice that you are sabotaging something for a long time, make it an intended sabotage, a strategic underachievement, instead of a blunt procrastination.

***

Don't let the day pass without something great. Be your own most desired experiment.

***

To make a difference, you must care enough to save time to make a difference.

***

It's never the best or the worst of times; time becomes what you make of it.

***

Intentional curiosity is the ability to deliberately direct your attention toward information inside or outside you. It is a skill. Use it generously.

***

Time is the ultimate status symbol.

***

Kevin Kelly said best: "Over the long term, the future is decided by optimists." No matter how comfortable the pessimistic state seems—optimize for optimism.

***

Time is the best friend when you stand on the ground of discipline and commitment. Time is the worst enemy when you don't know what ground you stand on. And all this time, the time is neutral.

***

It's better to do things that matter imperfectly rather than invest even a minute in things that don't matter.

***

Being future-ready isn't a luxury.

***

Right goals get you to dreams with the speed of light.

***

When, not if.

***

There's always a good reason not to begin. You're never perfectly ready. Just do it.

***

Using Software as a Service is a typical way to optimize for time. But the reverse, Service as a Software, is right around the corner. The faster you figure out how to use the reverse, the better.

***

Some ceilings are double glass, but you learn it only when you break the first layer. Make sure to plan for double resistance. Always.

***

The more-for-less mindset that doesn't value time will keep you from pursuing moonshots.

***

If you want to understand a topic, don't only read about it; write about it. It's well worth the time.

***

Best stories own time. Whoever has the best story and way to tell it—wins.

***

This is how to work on your goals: Pick a goal. Run like hell towards it. Then stop and figure out where you are. And then run again. Not an hour less, not an hour more.

***

Talent equals commitment, consistent efforts, plus decades of patience.

***

The key metric is the result, not hours. Long, hard-working hours won't feel like a must; instead, they will be a choice if you properly encourage and motivate yourself and the humans around you.

***

Choose habits that make you feel great at the moment and lead to the results you want in the long run.

***

Never underestimate the power of consistent work.

***

The time to reflect on your investment strategy is when you are most successful, not when everything is falling apart.

***

Discipline trains your mind to push through difficulty, dead ends, discomfort, and adversity. If it needs to get done, it gets done.

***

Investing shall become your daily habit. That's the only secret to investing.

***

The longer you wait, the harder it will be to change your established patterns and identity.

***

There's always a natural, most convenient investing time horizon, usually 10+ years. That's when markets reward your patience; the more your time horizon compresses, the more you rely on luck and tend to ruin everything.

***

Urgent things usually feel more urgent than they are. Give yourself time to figure out what deserves your urgent attention.

***

Big life changes need time and effort. Be patient and persistent, and you'll be amazed at the progress you can achieve within a year.

***

There's a time for complying, and there's a time for strategic rebellion.

***

You can build your dreams at any age and at any time.

***

There's no good or bad time—there's just the time in front of you right now, the time you'll never be able to live through again behind you, the time you don't know anything about yet ahead of you.

***

You can't grind all the time. And you don't need to. Take a break.

MONEY.

***

Money is white because it is plain. Simple. Transparent. A blank canvas full of opportunities. Its impact on your life is inevitable.

***

Money is white like the clean, crispy sheets, the first page of your new notebook, the first wedding dress, the snow, and the sand on Florida's Siesta Key.

***

To build wealth, you need to think of yourself as an investor. To start thinking like an investor, you must make peace with the basics: money is energy, energy is life, and life is you. Money is good. You are good.

***

Don't get rich instead—build wealth. To build wealth, consider the following: How much value do I create? How much of this value do I retain? How much leverage is being applied to my work? At what rate and for how long can I compound my capital?

***

When you reach the first solid foundation of wealth [about $1M], it's time to ask some new questions: How much money do I spend? How much is at risk of significant loss? How much am I giving back, i.e., returning to society? What shall I do with whatever capital I have left?

***

Wealth is patience applied intelligently.

***

If even talking about money is taboo, you will have no money.

***

Fear sells, but it doesn't pay.

***

Success in investing can require extreme patience. Create conditions that support patience and put the right systems in place [capital, cash flow, community, and expense systems].

***

You can't save your way to significant wealth.

***

Risk is what's left over after you think you've thought of everything.

***

Once you understand asymmetrical investing, you become addicted [in a positive way] to finding the next opportunity.

***

In markets, you buy your portfolio every day.

***

Instead of making the old product more efficient, invest time and money in building something new. Old products have patina; they are precious as they are. New products can take you to space.

***

If you figure out how to turn your product's use value into exchange value [social, cultural, environmental capital], you will win on many levels simultaneously.

***

So, what's your growth stack?

***

Unicorns die when caution turns into fear.

***

Cheap is always the most expensive option.

***

Create and give something right to the right humans at the right time for the right reasons. This is how you get rewarded greatly.

***

Your skill set is the only asset that can go up and to the right forever.

***

Any investment is a number from today multiplied by a story

about tomorrow.

***

The question is not: How can I avoid inefficiency? The question is: What is the optimal amount of inefficiency I can put up with to still function in a messy, imperfect world? Compounding runs on accepting the optimal level of hassle. It is fueled by endurance. So, sitting through periods of insanity is not a defect; it's accepting the optimal level of hassle.

***

If you decide to build a business, don't lose money on the name. Just pick the easiest one. The best brands take a meaningless word or name, like Disney, and fill it with meaning to evoke a positive emotional response to the product or service.

***

The comfort zone is where unicorns go to die.

***

Wealth compounding is quickly demolished by ego, lack of emotional intelligence, overconfidence, narrow focus, failure to correct mistakes fast or adjust to new circumstances, playing high-risk games without a competitive advantage, lacking financial resilience due to fragile financial foundation, and lacking personal resilience or burnout.

***

Make things better by making better things.

***

It pays back to build something great with no money other than not quite enough money.

***

Avoid style drifting into a game in which you don't have an edge.

***

There is a big gap between rich and wealthy.

***

If you can't imagine what the world would be like with your startup/project/business in it, it'll be triple hard to get off the starting line.

***

Humans want to buy very expensive things; they just need a very good reason. Don't be afraid to create the category of one & only.

***

Classic ingredients for bad decisions are ego, biases, emotions, and burnout.

***

What describes best where you are now:

1. You don't do what you want because you have no idea how to monetize it.
2. You do what you want but get way less profit than you want.
3. You do what you want and get as much profit as you want.
4. You have no idea what you want.
5. You must do what you don't want to do to get just enough.

6.   You do what you don't want to do and get much less than you want.

If you answered anything but 3., it's time to course correct. Fast.

***

Some humans are so poor that all they have is money.

***

If you can't explain how the company makes money in 1 minute, you probably shouldn't invest in it.

***

The easiest way to earn money—is to sell money.

***

Investing requires consistency. Your investing muscle evolves as you evolve.

***

Investing is not a game. It is a skill. You build it up by training yourself to understand the dynamics of financial markets, having a financial plan, creating a habit of watching the market with emotions turned off, and developing a risk management attitude.

***

Investing means doing something that might not work. It requires high self-esteem to start and to keep going.

***

Good design and good branding are almost always worth paying for.

***

Before you commit to building something new, ask yourself:

Does my new product or service hold more value to someone than what they're already focused on? If not, they're unlikely to switch their attention to what you want to build.

***

The more you bet, the more you win when you win.

***

Success is not what you can do; it's what you can do within the context of what your mind is willing to endure for the risk and reward in a given moment. Learn to respect risk.

***

You must cut out everything that doesn't matter to get good at your work. If you haven't figured out how to do that yet, you haven't aced at what you do [yet].

***

Why you do [or will] fear investing:

1. You might lose money.
2. You have a lack of knowledge.
3. You fear missing out.
4. You have a hard time managing your emotions.
5. You fear commitment.

Consider this: you'll inevitably experience one of two outcomes—either the weight of commitment or the sting of regret.

***

Never revenge. If you have a loss, push the brake and give yourself time to refine your investment skills.

***

If you're unwilling to invest in yourself, don't expect other humans to invest in you.

***

Fees and costs can eat into your investment returns. Be sure you understand all the costs associated with the investment, including broker fees, transaction fees, and management fees.

***

Things to do before you start investing—establish a positive cash flow, create an easily accessible cash safety net for six months for each of your immediate family members [no matter whether they are grown up or not], and cover the basics by writing down your financial plan.

***

Striking the right portfolio balance separates great investors from the rest.

***

Investing is more about emotions than money. The stock market behaves erratically in the short term—because our emotions affect its movement.

***

The beginner investor level: 80% index fund + 10% high-risk assets + 10% random new investments.

***

The professional investor level: 50% index fund + 30% high-risk assets + 20% random new investments.

***

The ace investor level: stick with what you already know works best for you.

***

If you want to invest with the fund but don't know about <u>the Medallion Fund</u>, you'd better learn more about it faster because it is the level you should strive for.

***

Key investing concepts you must know for building wealth: allocation [how much of what you shall own], overlapping positions [if you decide to invest in multiple funds], and tax efficiency.

***

The best marketing lowers the imagination barrier. It's worth investing in.

***

Before you start investing, make optimism your default.

***

You don't need to lose a lot to win a lot; there is no such ratio. Also, you don't simply win—you build and create.

***

Remember that even the best early-stage investors expect to lose money on more than 50% of their deals.

***

Most great investments begin in discomfort.

***

For every idea you think is unique, investors have heard several pitches. Be unique squared.

***

If you can show investors the big vision backed by data, team, and expertise, they'll invest in you.

***

If you aim to be an investor, you shouldn't care about the short term. If you want to be a trader—you should.

***

Pessimism sometimes sells; optimism consistently earns.

***

Your investment portfolio shall be diversified enough to survive and concentrated enough to matter.

***

If you want to invest in startups and not lose money, here's what you need to consider before moving forward: long-term defensibility; excellent, fast team; significant economic moat; initial market; realistic valuation; breakthrough product.

***

Rule #1: pay yourself first.

***

For financial freedom, you must take risks. There's no way around it; don't waste time searching.

***

When you try to be your target audience, you mess things up [99% of the time].

***

Five simple investing insights:

1. If you have freedom, you have wealth [not the other way around].

2. Complexity doesn't mean better returns.

3. The best way to face risk is to save more money.

4. The best passive investing strategy is dollar-cost averaging.

5. Stay away from what you don't understand.

***

No matter what you want to do in your career, you must approach it as a business. It's also smart to approach your passion from a business perspective.

***

If you want to build something valuable and profitable, consider what humans do, not what they say.

***

It wasn't all e-commerce, then it wasn't all blockchain, now it isn't all AI things that raise big rounds, the next big thing will not be all as well—find your thing, stick to it, grow it.

***

Investing gives you the rare opportunity to taste life twice—in the moment and at the exit.

***

Don't just earn money—strive to be financially unbreakable. Create wealth, protect it, and manage it.

***

Achieving wealth follows a simple roadmap: produce value, seize opportunities, leverage resources, persevere, and compound. Losing wealth follows a simple roadmap: don't master emotional control or learn to face rapid change, over-consume, catastrophize, and be rigid.

***

The most important things in life compound value from patience and deficit. Patience compounds growth, and deficit compounds appreciation for what it grows into.

***

Financial freedom should not be a dream but a deliberately calculated destination.

***

Saving your first $100K is an important personal milestone. Celebrate it.

***

The more you grow personally, the more your wealth will grow eventually.

***

Progress requires pessimism and optimism to coexist. Save like a pessimist; invest like an optimist.

***

Falling stock prices scare humans, which causes them to short, which makes prices fall, which scares more humans, which causes more humans to short, and so on. It works both ways.

***

You say you are great, but how does greatness show up in your financials?

***

Focus on things that don't change—this is how you build the most robust investment portfolio.

***

The goal isn't more money. The goal is to live life on your terms.

***

Ace investors do two things that others don't: actively seek information or views that challenge and contradict their own and maintain flexibility in their beliefs, especially when the evidence suggests they should.

***

Compounding works slowly, then ferociously. The mere thought of it works best against impatience.

***

There may be nothing across the entire spectrum of human endeavor that makes so many smart humans feel so stupid as investing does.

***

Money can be made in the present by mining the past, future, or both.

***

Money is fluid. Its value only becomes realized when it's put into motion. Therefore, money is a reflection of your values and intentions.

***

Investing requires an understanding of both fear and greed. As you progress in your investment journey, you learn how to push these emotions into conscious awareness, and, as a result, you learn to manage them better.

***

When you invest, be okay with losing, but never lose big. Never lose more than 10% of your investment. This is the threshold you can always bounce back from.

***

Invest in things that gain value or regularly pay you back in cash to grow your wealth. Ideally, of course, they will have both. That's all there is to investing and all the books written about it.

***

Pick an investment strategy that fits your personality. Once you've done your research and made your decision, you must trust your strategy wholeheartedly. If you find it hard to explain your investment strategy in 1 minute, take it as a sign to do more research. The goal is to confidently articulate your investment strategy and the reasons behind your decisions.

***

You live in the creative economy [right now, at least]. And in the creative economy, the story is the currency.

***

Wealth is now a factor of education, innovation, network, and the rule of law.

***

Ensure your investment decisions match your financial goals and how you want to live. There shall be no compromise on any.

***

Mark Suster said best: "Invest in lines, not dots," no matter what or who you want to invest in. The lines are not supposed to be perfectly straight, and the dots can sometimes become lines, so you should know which dot to keep an eye on.

***

Never invest all your funds. Investing isn't gambling. It's about making calculated decisions based on research and analysis.

***

Size matters. Yes, money can't motivate you. Yes, very big money can.

***

Market timing is a myth. Hold your equity through the ups and downs. No matter what, don't talk yourself out of investing. It's too valuable to pass up. Over time, markets generally go up. You either ride the wave or miss out.

***

Someone somewhere right now is building something that will utterly change the future—your goal here is not to find them but to determine the market where the innovation will land and be among the first to invest.

***

You will only know what investing feels like once you take your money and put it on the line.

***

You are here for a profit. And you deserve every single bit of it.

***

Building wealth is an honorable goal.

STATUS.

***

Status is blue because it is reliable. Trustworthy. Calm. Vast like the Milky Way. Its impact on your life is inevitable.

***

Status is blue and borderless like the sky; like the cornflower, it is vulnerable; like the water, it can move mountains.

***

To compound status means to think long-term.

***

Even if you don't think you're a participant in the game of status, you are.

***

When you woke up today, what did you tell yourself?

***

The best companies are cool. To be cool, you need a great product, of course; that's table stakes. But beyond that, savvy companies craft brands that become associated, first, with status.

***

When building status—do not strive for linearity.

***

Say what you want, know what you need. Also, know your enough.

***

You can't get rid of status. Monks have status. Nuns do, too. As a species, we're uniquely adept at taking any slight advantage and turning it into a status marker.

***

Status isn't static. It used to be high status to be overweight.

***

Every choice you make is a statement on status—even if the statement is that you [supposedly] don't care about status.

***

The more experienced you are, the more you are tempted to fit any new situation into your existing world model and status. To succeed, you must accumulate a mental database of case studies but refrain from drawing simplistic lessons or clinging to them too tightly.

***

All financial and product bubbles are driven by status.

***

Status can also be a SaaS—Status as a Service.

***

The neighbors of lottery winners end up buying fancier cars even if they can barely afford them. That fact alone shall tell you a lot about the power of status.

***

Wanting to belong can and will kill your genius.

***

Failure doesn't break you. It builds you. After every failure, you don't start from scratch; you start with experience.

***

Your perception is your reality. There's also a real reality. But it is an entirely different story.

***

How you allow anything to affect you is your superpower.

***

Black tie is a convention because it's a chosen practice loaded with meaning. First, you need meaning, and then you get status.

***

Understanding status helps you understand the culture and predict what comes next in business and life.

***

Do what you say you are going to do, and your status will compound.

***

The definition of luxury is quality of life in every aspect, including your investment portfolio, your living arrangements, your habits and hobbies, your brand, your network, the culture you have access to, your taste, and your mental and physical health.

***

You don't inherit yourself. You create yourself. And sometimes, you need to rediscover yourself.

***

When you don't trust yourself, you outsource your worth to others.

***

Extreme success requires extreme sacrifice. Don't make this sacrifice unconsciously. Also, don't mind that it hurts. Endure the pain when necessary rather than looking for shortcuts.

***

The more growth you have, the more change you get. It compounds.

***

If you train yourself to see big patterns and opportunities, you're unlikely to make a bad choice.

***

You will never be great if you don't have the patience to be average for a while.

***

No marketing will save you from bad quality. The bad quality will give you a bad name. Watch it.

***

No amount of tactical progress can make up for strategic misjudgment. In other words, you can be moving fast—that's progress, but you can be moving in the wrong direction—that's strategic misjudgment.

***

Success means you will have better, bigger, more exciting problems. Rejoice.

***

You perform to the level of your self-image. Always.

***

If you want to progress in any area, you need to be willing to give up your best ideas occasionally.

***

You have to move as fast as you can just to stay where you are, and to get somewhere significantly better, you have to move at least twice as fast. This is actually true.

***

There are two types of status: temporary and expired. Very often, they intermingle.

***

Your job is to accept and admire yourself first. The acceptance and admiration from others will follow. Not vice versa.

***

Don't dread comparisons—leverage them. If you are not being compared to anyone, you are somewhere in between or past.

***

When you know who you are and are content to be yourself, neither comparing nor competing, but getting what you want, everyone will respect you.

***

Deliberately. Practice. Doing. Hard. Things. This is how you unlock greatness.

***

Failure also means not trying something you want to do because you can't accept not achieving the expected outcome.

***

You won't be able to make better decisions before you understand the rationale behind your previous decisions. If you don't know how you got "here," you risk making things much worse.

***

Status success has its own 4P formula: Purpose, Patience, Passion, and Perseverance.

***

No one can define success for you but you.

***

Build a brand, not just a business.

***

Authenticity means danger. Beware and go for it.

***

Your business is a stepping stone, not a final destination. It shall always be this way. Craft it to wield financial benefit and a distinct advantage that quickly propels you forward. How can your existing business serve as a catalyst, a pivotal link, or a gateway to something new and much bigger?

***

The most significant risks are always the same, yet different.

***

You suddenly become more powerful, interesting, and attractive once you have fun with life.

***

Mental toughness is persistence, not intensity.

***

The skill of second-order thinking is an ultimate advantage—it is the practice of not just considering the consequences of your decisions but also the consequences of those consequences.

***

You don't need to be a high performer, but you need to be interesting.

***

Sometimes, your memory can become an obstacle. This is how humans become afraid of risk, new ventures, and growth in general. Don't let this be you.

***

Deliver impact that lasts—that's how you build up businesses, networks, and, eventually, status.

***

"Competition is for losers," as Peter Thiel has said. What you need are defensibility and differentiation.

***

Macrofocus means to understand what is essential. Microfocus means always remembering it. One without the other can lead to great losses. Combining both with consistent effort unlocks an unstoppable you.

***

The market does not need to be persuaded; you must have something to show it.

***

Problems happen when you compromise your values, boundaries, and principles.

***

The Latin word for business is *negotium*. To run a business at a high level, you must master negotiation skills. Your status is proportionate to the level you can run a business.

***

Create a life system that will keep backing your sustainable growth even when you sleep.

***

Your strategic curiosity is what sets you apart from others in your field.

***

When it's time to make a choice, ask yourself: Does this choice diminish or elevate me? How does it help me grow?

***

You can live if you don't understand the "why" or the "how," but you can't live a good life.

***

Don't mistake someone else's insecurities for your abilities.

***

If you notice during the conversation that the other party is manipulating or trying to provoke you, say, "Let me stop right here."

***

You break promises to others because you break promises to yourself. The question you have in mind is, "If I don't deserve my commitment, then why should others?". But you deserve commitment. And others deserve it, too.

***

Real progress is inherently disruptive; it doesn't happen on demand or when convenient.

***

Too much, too soon, too fast—a good thing on steroids quickly becomes a bad thing. Don't speed up the status-building process beyond what you can handle.

***

Work can [even more shall] be a choice, not a necessity.

***

What personal and professional growth metrics are you tracking? If you don't track any metrics, you have a mess in your head, and your results will match it. Double down on focus and prioritization if you have too many metrics. Are the metrics you've chosen really important or just convenient? You are not only what you repeatedly do but also what you repeatedly track.

***

When you start something meaningful, avoid secondary work at all costs—business processes optimization, market and user research, corporate structure refurbishing, software refactoring, speaking at various events, and showing off on social media. Instead, focus on two things: 1. Building a product humans love and 2. Achieving growth targets in a chosen time frame.

***

To win, you must have a true passion for the game. To decide whether to enter and stay in the game, you must deeply know yourself.

***

Your experience is not the same as your expertise.

***

Focus on knowledge over information.

***

Let others always share their opinions first. A strong opinion sways humans one way. You can't afford them to hear only your opinion.

***

When you say it twice—write it down. Avoid explaining the same thing over & over again at all costs.

***

To outperform anyone, your thinking has to be different and better.

***

Risk being wrong at least one time per day.

***

The base rate is just a statistic. And, sometimes, it is the success rate of everyone who's done what you're about to do.

***

Live a fulfilling life. Don't focus on getting rich or famous. Don't focus on getting admiration. Live your best life and help others around you do the same. Then, you will be wealthy, famous, and admired.

***

You are here to succeed, not to impress.

***

A great life requires a lot of uninterrupted focus. That means saying no to LLV [Low Life Value] things and concentrating on the few HLV [High Life Value] things.

***

Sometimes, you avoid growth because you don't want to deal with the emotional pain of that growth failing. This is called cutting yourself off from success.

***

When you avoid anything that could challenge your views, you become entangled in the Ostrich effect. Be aware of it and cut it out before it takes over.

***

There are many recipes for success. There are many ways to win. But all recipes include two ingredients: curiosity and integrity.

***

There is no human society without culture, and there is no culture without status.

***

Longevity is crucial to success. Take care of yourself.

***

Earn and deserve the success you want.

***

Efficiency alone doesn't build a generation-defining company.

***

What you know matters, but who you are matters more.

***

Nobody can make the difference you are meant to make for you.

***

You alone are [almost always] enough.

***

You don't grow old; you get old when you stop growing.

***

Life is not all about status, but a lot of life is about status.

***

The status you build will be the legacy you leave.

RELATIONSHIPS.

***

Relationships are black because they are complex. Multifaceted. Unpredictable. Resilient and strong, but at the same time fragile, like Earth. Their impact on your life is inevitable.

***

Black is the result of the complete absorption of visible light. Every color needs it for depth and variety. That's why relationships are black; they absorb everything and can give everything in return; they can suck in warmth and provide warmth, stop the growth, and help the growth.

***

Once the toothpaste is out of the tube, you can't put it back in. It's the same with relationships.

***

Often, it is just one big decision. Don't fuck it up.

***

Some relationships are doing great, most are doing okay, and some are doing little to nothing. Great is not forever, okay is not okay, nothing is a dead end. Determine where your most important relationships are, and course-correct accordingly.

***

How to connect with others: Share with someone who wants to listen or listen to someone who wants to share.

***

It's not about getting cheered when you open the door; that shall be normal. It's being noticed when you're gone that truly matters.

***

Too much communication signals that the relationship is not functioning well. Discussing everything non-stop is required only when a relationship [no matter professional or personal] doesn't flow naturally. When you notice this, go back to the basics, the pain, and what everyone is afraid to hear.

***

Don't offend your own sense of logic.

***

When you desire someone for what they might be, you are, in a way, rejecting them for the way they are.

***

Don't run from the pain of not being sure.

***

Make sure you give others what they need, and for this, use the 3H model: Do they want to be Heard, Helped, or Hugged? The answer to this question will help you avoid misunderstanding and conflict with pretty much anyone. Also, make sure to communicate what you need. And have enough self-respect not to accept anything else.

***

Anxiety stems from too much connectivity and too much comparison.

***

Cynicism is a defense mechanism. You show weakness when you use cynicism.

***

In any relationship, don't wait until feedback becomes bad news; give it when it can clarify.

***

The question is not: How can I earn the highest returns? The question is: What are the highest returns I can maintain over the long term? Goes for both investing and relationships.

***

Nobody will be happy being with you if you can't be happy with yourself.

***

Gratitude and feedback shall not only be in your mind.

***

A feeling is just a feeling—it's not your identity.

***

When you make choices, look for signs of excellence, not lack of weakness.

***

It's not enough to earn praise; you must deserve it. It's not enough to just be loved; you must be loveable.

***

In any relationship, focus on good consistency rather than absolute intensity.

***

No single person's craziness should grind your progress to a stop.

***

Coaching partnership isn't like school. It's not a checkbox to tick. This is a way to grow. Mentoring, too.

***

Whatever your excellence is, make it clear.

***

Money itself cannot make a great relationship, but the lack of it can mess one up.

***

For a relationship to thrive, it can't be used to fill the void or heal traumas. Your partner isn't there to fix you.

***

The only way to be truly confident in yourself is to become comfortable with what you lack.

***

Never bet against other human's progress.

***

At the core of every society are the key collective values and goals. Your society must match your values and goals [not vice versa]. If you find yourself in a "push-adjust" position, you are in the wrong place at the right time.

***

The cost of making decisions to please others instead of focusing on your own growth is misery.

***

Detachment isn't about not feeling; it's about making the right decision despite misleading feelings.

***

Aim to work for interesting companies, become friends with interesting humans, or build a company that engages interesting humans in solving important problems.

***

Anger helps with loss, self-doubt, and powerlessness. But to get back at the other is not how you get the other back.

***

The happiest relationships involve two [or more] humans who know how to be happy alone.

***

It is not someone else's responsibility to create the conditions for your success and happiness. It's on you.

***

Care for humans, genuinely care. And if you choose not to care, then be ready not to receive care in return.

***

You'll never meet someone who doesn't have a good idea somewhere inside. This includes you.

***

Listen for intent and expectations, not for words.

***

If you have too many anchors in your relationship, you can either cut them off and move on or sink the ship and move on. You can't progress or even budge with anchors weighing you down.

***

Pick a partner, not a firm. This applies to all professional relationships, regardless of the context.

***

Humans only need logic to justify their emotional decisions. You are human.

***

Clarity saves relationships.

***

In relationships, be a researcher. Experiment fearlessly, often, and together.

***

There's a situationship, and then there's a relationship. Make sure you know the difference.

***

The best thing you can keep doing over and over again is to stop expecting yourself from other humans.

***

Delegate responsibility, not tasks.

***

You can win an argument but lose a relationship. You can lose an argument but win a relationship. You can have no arguments if you resolve them before they have the chance to happen; this is how you win a relationship over and over again. It's up to you.

***

Innocence isn't lost—it is traded for wisdom.

***

Curiosity eliminates resistance.

***

The scarcest commodity is integrity. In every relationship, optimize for integrity.

***

It's better to be interesting than likable.

***

Relationships are euphoric when they start, but they only become good when you work on them continuously for a long time.

***

The only thing most humans try to protect you from is happiness.

***

The whole point of risk in anything, including relationships, is that you don't know.

***

The best salespeople are often horrible managers, and vice versa.

***

Being together is important, but you must have a solo safe place for brave ideas.

***

What you do on your worst day is impossible to fake. You're only as good as how you choose to show up on your worst day.

***

Eventually, all you love and care for you will lose, but it will be back to you later in a different form.

PEACE OF MIND.

***

Peace of mind has no color. Because it's everything everywhere all at once, it's beyond the physical realm, yet it depends on it. It is contentment, clarity, serenity, and harmony. Its impact on your life is inevitable.

***

Peace of mind is a gap between good and as good as it can be.

***

"Get Your Own" used to be the name of my Wi-Fi back in 2012. It also served as a reminder to get my own investment portfolio, nice things, books, cars, clothes, houses, groceries, inspiration, experiences, lessons, notebooks, and peace of mind.

***

If you want to predict the future, stop; instead, do the POP [Positioning Over Predicting]. You can't predict the future, but you can position yourself for peace of mind for multiple possible futures. You must adapt to all futures rather than plan for a single desired.

***

Life is an experiment. And growth isn't something you can finish.

***

Your problem is [usually] not at all what you are trying to improve.

***

Change yourself; change someone; ignore everyone.

***

When someone accuses you of being selfish, remember that in some cases, it is true, but in most cases, they are upset only because you aren't doing what they selfishly want you to do.

***

Usually, you talk about what you do and what you want to do too early to find excuses not to do it.

***

You either stall by making excuses or rise high by making a difference.

***

All frameworks are incomplete, but some are useful.

***

Choose that which gives you the freedom to live and to leave on your terms.

***

Cultivate strategic indifference to things outside your control.

***

Don't be backward about going forward.

***

What lifestyle feels ideal for you most of the time? Build that.

***

When you start working on something new, until you have more context for deciding what to work on first, for two weeks, just write things down.

***

To make the world a better place, you don't need to make everything better. To change—you don't have to change everything.

***

You don't do something great because you feel like it; you start feeling like it because you start doing something great and meaningful.

***

Your peace of mind rises to the level that you accept.

***

Inner safety exists only in vulnerability.

***

Overthinking is as debilitating as not thinking at all.

***

Procrastination is not rest. Period.

***

Sit down and do it until it's done. This is how you maintain peace of mind.

***

What do you sound like when you sound like you?

***

There's nothing wrong with wrong decisions. They are part of life. However, to make them work anyway is what can make you successful.

***

You can lose everything, more than you thought possible, and still spring back stronger than you've ever been.

***

Fill the void with acceptance and knowledge, not stuff.

***

If you observe your thoughts carefully, you'll notice that only one of every five thoughts is useful.

***

Trying hard to push thoughts away makes them stick around longer and shout louder in your mind. Instead of suppressing—accept your thoughts, let them move through you, but never let them stop.

***

If you need things to be a certain way, you are held hostage by them.

***

Meaningful change happens exponentially.

***

Some things have to be believed to be seen.

***

The future is vital. The past is important. But if you lose the present, you lose everything.

***

Fear is the natural response you get when moving closer to the truth. Internal resistance points directly to the significance of your actions. Conversely, choices devoid of resistance lack opportunities for growth, challenge, or valuable lessons.

***

You start being a happy human the day you stop pretending to be one.

***

Peace of mind stands on integrity, intention, and not taking yourself too seriously.

***

When there's too much uncertainty, push through the grind and maintain the momentum instead of stopping.

***

You make yourself miserable, not just by railing against bad experiences or craving experiences you aren't having, but by trying too hard to hold onto the good experiences you are currently having. Learn to let go.

***

Freedom without structure can feel limiting. But the good thing about life is that you get to set your own structure.

***

What if, after you are gone, your only choice is to repeat the life you are living right now? Would you be eager to repeat the same life? If not, it's time for a change.

***

Want to know the actual state of your peace of mind? Read something you fiercely disagree with on the internet.

***

Never outsource what you enjoy.

***

Don't look to anyone else to make a good life for you; this you must do for yourself.

***

More important problems usually hide behind less important problems. Don't fool yourself by solving just the less important ones.

***

Both extraordinary results and peace of mind are a consequence of doing the work, not the other way around.

***

Never negotiate with yourself. Compete with yourself—yes, but never negotiate.

***

Life is all about managing probabilities.

***

Not acting is a decision.

***

If you begin, you must keep on beginning.

***

Minding your peace of mind might not be a piece of cake, but it is your own. You got it, and it's worth it.

FINAL NOTES

Note 1. Good things in life are about 1+1=2.

Note 2. Great things in life are about 1+1=3 [where 3 is value and leverage: time, money, status, relationships, peace of mind].

Note 3. Nothing in this book is financial advice.

Note 4. Be a smart human and take responsibility for your choices. Life offers no guarantees. Conduct your thorough research before making any financial or investment decisions. Your commitments shape your results, and both are your responsibility.

Note 5. Don't forget that T.M.S.R.P. is designed to be accessible on your phone, tablet, computer, or table around the clock. You can copy out the pieces that resonate most with you, work with them, develop and improve them, and make them your own. It doesn't matter at what page you start—it works bottom up and top down. Whether you're gearing up for a TED talk, a pitch competition, a tough conversation, an annual performance review, whether a difficult decision lies ahead of you or an exhausting negotiation behind you, whether you're reassessing your business strategy, investment plans, personal or professional relationships, or just want to get to know yourself better—

T.M.S.R.P. is your reliable guide.

Note 6. Yes, note 5 repeats the last paragraph from "Instructions for use" because sometimes a friendly reminder is all we need.

BIG AND SPECIAL THANKS

Big thanks to the world's most generous Clients, Partners, Mentors, & Friends from Tesla, Amazon, Google, McKinsey & Company, Uber, Forbes, Y Combinator, Techstars, Yale School of Management, London Business School, Kellogg School of Management, Massachusetts Institute of Technology, University of Chicago Booth School of Business, Institute of Coaching, McLean/Harvard Medical School, & U.S. Air Force for quality-proofing drafts of this book.

Thank you for intelligent sparring, earnestness, inspiration, helpful suggestions, careful corrections, continuous feedback, smart questions, for reminding me that I shall not take myself too seriously, for your ongoing interest, for many glimpses into the future, and of course, for believing in me.

Special thanks to you, *dear M.*

THE VERY FINAL NOTE

It's time for us to part. Before we do that, I'd like to remind you that it's okay to fall short and not live up to every one of three hundred sixty-five pieces of wisdom.

Make mistakes. But keep this guide accessible on your phone, tablet, computer, or table around the clock. Its task is to help you make better mistakes better.

You won't get everything right, but you already know that being right is not the point.

Make progress. Sometimes incremental, sometimes skyrocketing, but only in things that matter.

Just because something, some piece of wisdom from this guide, isn't working for you right now, consider that maybe right now is not the best time for it, maybe right now you need to double down on saving money for it, maybe right now your status is stalling and needs a hand, maybe right now your relationships require your immediate attention, maybe right now you are negotiating with yourself too much, and your mind is screaming for peace.

After all, you are not *only* human; you are *the only* human. You can do it. You got it.

APPENDIX 1

MILLION DOLLAR COACH PLAYBOOK [MDCP]

Dear reader, below, you will find valuable pieces of wisdom from the Million Dollar Coach Playbook [MDCP], released in 2021.

***

You don't need to be madly in love with humans to become a Million Dollar Coach.

What you need is:

Genuine Integrity—to remain calm & balanced.

Radical Discipline—to go if you need to.

Strategic Consistency—to keep all parties accountable.

Passionate Curiosity—to dig deeper.

Courageous Vulnerability—to accept humans as they are and be present as you are.

***

As a Million Dollar Coach [MDC], your expected impact on the world is a force defined by two key elements: trajectory and scale.

***

Direction is what you choose to work on. The most important thing to keep in mind when you choose your direction is trust—you have to trust yourself when others don't see what you see.

***

What coaching area to choose:

1. Life—the most comprehensive & complex area.
2. Executive and Career—more definitive than Life, yet still have a lot of variables.
3. Relationships—this area is a big part of Life.
4. Success + Leadership + Habits + Negotiations—these areas are valuable parts of Life yet can be explored independently.
5. Business + Startup—these are the areas with an emphasis on group/team success.
6. Health + Wellness—a distinctive part of Life; they require additional coaching training.

Additional coaching areas worth considering are Productivity, Accountability, Monetization, Investment, Retirement, Creative Thinking, Time Management, Happiness, Curiosity, and Public Speaking.

***

The fact that you want to become a Million Dollar Coach means that you shall be profound at & evolving further in the areas most problematic for your Clients—not just in coaching.

***

When you want to join the club, the main idea to keep in mind while making a choice is that your Clubs shall be a part of the system, meaning they absolutely must add value to your coaching practice in terms of new Clients, meaningful conversations, educational tools, and ad-hoc professional advice.

***

Your social media success is not limited to or guaranteed by the choice of the profile picture & executive summary. The main idea is that you don't need all the world's fans; you need a group of committed fans who might as well follow you on different platforms.

***

When you communicate in any form, apply a method of reverse judgment—challenge yourself to imagine a picture where some more evolved and more exquisite version of your idea, product, or service works.

***

Your fee is the quintessence of your professional expertise, education, and hard & soft skills invested per Client for a certain period.

***

The underlying idea of your financial strategy shall be your Client's investment with purpose, their ROI, and your profit with purpose.

***

New Client acquisition is hardly possible without a solid, tested system:

80% of New Clients are attracted via the trusted referral line.

8% via web resources.

6% via Professional Organizations for Coaches.

4% via professional brokerage service.

2% by some random luck.

***

While expanding your Client List, remember:

Million Dollar Coach talks less and listens more.

Million Dollar Coach doesn't impose information; she asks questions.

Million Dollar Coach doesn't push ideas; she generates ideas from Clients.

Million Dollar Coach doesn't overshare her story; she taps into the Client's experience.

Million Dollar Coach doesn't present solutions; she expands the Client's thinking.

Million Dollar Coach doesn't give one-sided recommendations; she empowers Clients to choose.

***

Impostor syndrome = glass ceiling = comfort zone. And everything you want to be is on the other side of it.

***

You might think, "Who am I?" Well, you're a personality with a voice! Never assume you're less than any other human. The only difference between you and the one who is already succeeding is that they broke the glass ceiling, stepped out of their comfort zone & are on the path to becoming a Million Dollar Coach. In other words, they acted on their skill.

***

If you met someone exactly like yourself [same experience, same resources, same problems], what advice would you give them?

***

As you continue the coaching path, you will meet snobby C-level professionals, posh middle managers, overstressed startup founders, and desperately striving individuals who will reject your service.

They are going to give confusing directions & change their minds after you fulfill your commitments. It comes with the territory, my friend. Don't overthink; instead, laugh it off!

However, if you work with committed to growth humans and never stop upgrading yourself, you will encounter narrow-mindedness less & less.

Eventually, you will build a trusted circle of self-aware bright personalities that will pave the way for more grateful Clients to your door.

APPENDIX 2

MILLION DOLLAR INVESTOR PLAYBOOK
[MDIP]

Dear reader, below, you will find valuable pieces of wisdom from the Million Dollar Investor Playbook [MDIP], released in 2021.

***

Become an investor not because you need it but because you want it.

***

To become an investor, you must possess [and develop further] the following five qualities:

Curiosity—to figure out the unknown.

Flexibility—to accept any outcome.

Integrity—to align your decisions with your values.

Assertiveness—to not hide what you really want.

Courage—to never give up.

***

Your very first step on the way to "I am a Million Dollar Investor [MDI]" shall be a thorough self-assessment. You and only you can determine if you have the above qualities and know how to put them to work. Be the harsh judge; don't let yourself be blinded by your ego.

***

There's no shortcut to smart. Before becoming a smart, purpose-driven investor, you must pass the stage of a mediocre, lost investor. Remember—smart investors are not born in a blue ocean; they are built in a very red one.

***

Before you start investing, you need to:
Determine your investment purpose.
Organize your finances.

***

When choosing your investment area[s], apply the method of divergent thinking to create multiple investment baskets, and remember—an asset's illiquidity does not speak to its return potential.

***

There are two ways you can invest in startups.
Directly—as a founder, co-founder, or team member of a startup, as a knowledgeable and trustworthy solo angel investment partner.
Jointly—with a fund or within an angel investment syndicate, coop, incubator, accelerator, university innovation hub, or equity crowdfunding platform.

***

One important rule to remember while investing in startups is to invest like it's your startup.

***

To succeed in startup investing, you need a strong network that consistently provides helpful information.

***

Investment karma works because iterations are consistent. As an MDI, you shall aim to make your iterations within a well-thought, reliable, consistent, and compounding interest system.

***

Investing is not about idealism and perfectionism. It is about perseverance and understanding risk. Without these two, it's impossible to be a long-term successful investor.

***

When you make your first investment—you break the ground. When you make your second investment—you create a system. Your third and all the following investment decisions either contribute to this system or subtract from it.

***

To become an MDI, you must do things other investors don't like or want to do [i.e., long-term thinking, trend watching, profound research, value-matching, etc.].

***

If you are facing an investment choice and can't decide, the answer is no.

***

The OODA Loop [Observe, Orient, Decide, Act] works because it provides the advantage of speed, it helps you befriend the uncertainty, which eventually becomes comfortable if you have the right filters in place, and it teaches you how to leverage unpredictability for your benefit.

***

Complex investment relationships are not limited to those with other humans; they include relationships with your social media accounts, assets and liabilities, and your physical, mental, and spiritual development. All the above are investments of time, energy, and money.

***

When you make your first step towards becoming an MDI, you seek "freedom to"—freedom to afford more and better, to travel without boundaries, and to live on your terms.

When you evolve as a sustainable MDI, you start seeking "freedom from"—freedom from unnecessary obligations, social appearances, and the need for promotion. In other words, you become unemployable [in the most positive way], antifragile, unfuckwithable, and unstoppable.

***

There are only two ways of living—the way of "unit" and the way of "union." You will know that you've become an MDI when you live the way where one investment decision in your system adds value to the other—also known as the true way of union.

APPENDIX 3

MILLION DOLLAR NEGOTIATOR PLAYBOOK
[MDNP]

Dear reader, below, you will find valuable pieces of wisdom from the Million Dollar Negotiator Playbook [MDNP], released in 2022.

***

Your first step to "I am a Million Dollar Negotiator [MDN]" shall be a thorough situation detachment. One of the biggest mistakes you can make is to believe that the initial demand of the other party correlates with their genuine interest.

***

To become an MDN, you must possess [and develop further] the following five qualities:

Focused Curiosity—to open your mind to one new possibility at a time.

Intentional Detachment—to observe from all available perspectives.

Sustainable Integrity—to stay the course aligned with your values.

Second-Order Thinking—to understand the rationale behind previous decisions.

Active Listening & Hearing—to determine what is not being said, though it needs to be heard.

***

A true MDN knows how to switch from "what is relevant to me" to "what is relevant to all." She builds a path to winning by building trust, gaining commitment, and managing opposition.

***

To enter the arena of mid-level negotiations, you don't need to go through entry-grade levels, yet you need a portfolio of standard-level negotiations at a minimum of five during the last twelve months; a solid reference list at a minimum of ten reliable contacts; fluency in at least one of the languages spoken around a mid-level negotiation table you strive to sit at; clear schedule and readiness for ad hoc travel.

***

To enter the arena of high-level negotiations, you need all the above + a portfolio of mid-level negotiations at a minimum of five during the last twelve months.

***

Here are the types of negotiations you will encounter as a startup founder: negotiations with co-founders, negotiations with the first ten employees, negotiations with the team, negotiations with partners, negotiations with investors, negotiations with your life partner & family members since the startup tends to consume most of your life [especially during the first 24 months after the launch]. Are you ready to ace all the above?

***

As a startup founder, you may naturally tend to be impatient. However, in negotiations, impatience is nothing less than a weakness. Remember, patience is not passive; on the contrary, it is concentrated strength.

***

You don't find negotiation Clients—you create them.

***

It takes knowledge to gain knowledge. Therefore, you must profile your potential Clients ahead of time. Lay down on paper or in a digital format their likes/dislikes, social norms/causes they support, religious views, idea generation process, cultural belonging, geographical savviness, family status, etc. There's nothing inappropriate in prelim profiling; this is how you train yourself to know your audience, your humans.

***

Winning means fulfilling mutual needs while being consistent with your beliefs & values. It means finding out what the other party wants and showing them how to get it while you get what you want.

***

When you prepare for a negotiation, prepare not to beat the other party but to influence their decision-making in a way that will benefit both.

***

To powerfully conclude the negotiation, you must plan ahead; plan how you will gain sufficient investment in the process, furnish a basis for comparison, use the concession rate to signal the best deal, and after obtaining involvement, provide options or choices [humans tend to support that which they help create].

***

As an MDN, measure your satisfaction with the result by two criteria:

1. Was the process fair and just? Did the other party listen to what I had to say and respect my point of view?

2. How close did the final agreement come to satisfying my needs, interests, and expectations?

***

During the negotiation, you must make your decisions accurately, and for this, you apply the CCP rule, which stands for Clear, Credible, and Persuasive. Use this rule to assess your decision on the spot, and if even a slight doubt occurs, park the decision and move on with a pause [which, of course, is a decision in itself].

***

When you make decisions during the negotiation, make sure to analyze the logic behind the other party's decisions from four perspectives: Economic [price, performance, utility, routine, information], Social [status, belonging, memberships, clubs, fans], Cultural [rarity, distinction, community, cults, a hero story], Symbolic [meaning, history, worship, religion, immortality].

When you prepare, make your decisions hard to analyze from these four perspectives.

***

To be an MDN, you must be a great storyteller.

***

If negotiating were easy, everyone would be winning. The main lesson is that building a serious negotiation project portfolio requires earnest decisions. This is something most humans don't stress enough, but you should.

***

When you choose your Clients, you automatically choose their needs. There are five basic layers of human needs: physiological, safety, belonging and love, esteem, and self-actualization. Make sure you select the needs you want to help them meet.

***

3 is your most reliable number to keep in mind. You create 3 Clients at the very beginning. You label by repeating the last three words of the other party's previous sentence. You always have the chance to change the negotiation flow by changing an original statement by 3%. When you reach 3 of anything—pause.

***

Negotiation is a perishable skill. Your choices for your ability are in only one of four places: to be better, to be the same, to be worse, or not to be. So, when it's time for your next life-changing moment, will you be able to negotiate for it?

APPENDIX 4

THE ADAM METHOD
[TAM]

An integral coaching and mentoring method based on the power of microsteps, the principles of positive psychology, and neuroscience.

A—Articulate the goal.

D—Determine current reality, challenges, and obstacles.

A—Assess the range of potential solutions.

M—Move onward & upward with the best solution acting one microstep at a time.

The Adam Method [TAM] is rooted in essentialism, a disciplined approach to identifying what truly matters and cutting out everything else, allowing you to focus on making the greatest impact on the most important things.

It is designed to help you create a balanced, happy, wealthy, and sustainable life.

What

1.   Tailored Approach: It is designed to meet the specific needs of the Client.

2. Active Listening: The Coach/Mentor actively listens to understand the Client's needs and goals.

3. Empathy: The Coach/Mentor demonstrates empathy and understanding toward the Client's experiences and emotions.

4. Goals and Objectives: The focus is on helping the Client achieve their goals and objectives.

5. Actionable Feedback: The Coach/Mentor provides clear and actionable feedback that helps the Client improve and grow.

6. Continuous Growth: The focus is on continuous improvement, encouraging the Client to strive for excellence.

7. Evidence-Based: The method is based on research and evidence and is continuously updated to reflect the latest developments in the field.

8. Supportive Environment: The method creates a supportive and positive environment that encourages growth and development.

9. Sustainability: The method is designed to be sustainable and long-lasting, promoting ongoing growth and development beyond the coaching/mentoring relationship.

How

TAM Coaching & Mentoring—jumpstart your journey toward a balanced, happy, wealthy, & sustainable living + get valuable advice & insights in realms of time, money, status, relationships, and peace of mind via a signature individual or group 3/13-month program.

TAM Journal—start living a sustainable integral lifestyle by utilizing a digital guide with valuable advice & prompts for your health, wealth, and habits that work.

TAM Sky Coaching & Mentoring—speed up by slowing down in the trustworthy space of a single-engine plane, followed by an hour-long conversation where you can focus, clear your mind, gain perspective, and act.

At the heart of TAM is a proven track record of changing organizations and changing lives. The power of TAM has already changed over 50 organizations and over 2000 lives for the better.

TAM embraces the principles of executive coaching, expert mentoring, smart investing, strategic negotiating, and superior piloting.

TAM is both demanding and supportive. It pushes you to new heights, and it also has your back.

TAM Journey Milestones:
1. Confidence
2. Growth
3. Energy
4. Success
5. Excitement

Why

Scaling your life, business, or relationships starts with scaling your mind, so I built the Method I wished existed when I started.

TAM has been purpose-built for growth from day one.

Enhancing your navigational skills toward success can significantly speed up your progress. This has a dual benefit: the journey becomes shorter, and you can move faster with the certainty that you're on the right path. Much of TAM's value lies in providing the extra focus and confidence needed to accelerate.

Speed defines growth.
Focus & confidence enable speed.
TAM uplevels focus & confidence.
You win.

APPENDIX 5

THE ADAM CURVE
[TAC]

What

The idea behind The Adam Curve is future-proofed. Every coach can [but not necessarily does] go through four main stages of development. Research shows that 90% of startups fail. So do 90% of coaches. But they don't necessarily become bankrupt. Instead, they succumb to the safety of linear growth.

How

If you want to become an Ace Coach and don't understand how to do it fast, your best choice is to invest in working with an Ace Coach. It is simply the fastest way up.

Why

To become a coach, you must know what is possible. A coach can go from Aspiring to Ace by mastering five essential pillars: time, money, status, relationships, and peace of mind. If a coach masters only the first two [time and money], they will remain stuck on the Professional stage. If they find the courage to master the other three [status, relationships, and peace of mind], they will accelerate to Ace.

Now. Please meet TAC.

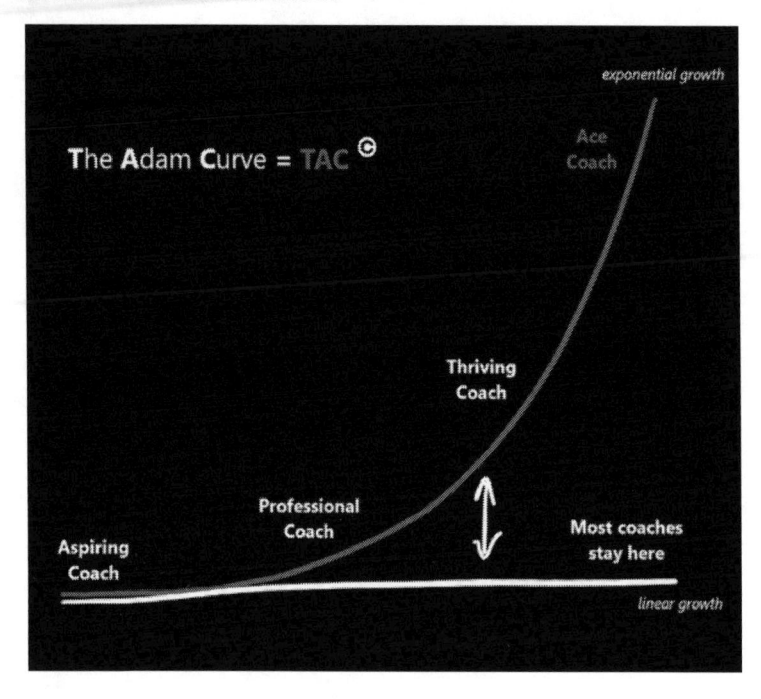

The Adam Curve = TAC ⊕

exponential growth

Ace Coach

Thriving Coach

Professional Coach

Aspiring Coach

Most coaches stay here

linear growth

APPENDIX 6

MY LIFE SYSTEM WORKSHEET
[MLSW]

My Life System in 12 steps.

Step 1. My Work

Take a large sheet of white paper and a black pen, then write your name in the center. Circle your name. Put the 1st arrow from your name up—"My Work." Under it, in a bullet point style, add actions you will take this year to enhance your professional position within the next ten years.

Step 2. My Personal & Professional Expression

Put the 2nd arrow from your name—"My Personal & Professional Expression." Under it, in a bullet point style, add clubs, organizations you are/want to become a member of, media you write/want to start writing/interviewing for, and social media platforms where you are/want to build your personal brand. These are key activities with a focus on this year and the potential to enhance your personal brand and professional position within the next ten years.

Step 3. My Events

Put the 3rd arrow from your name—"My Events." Under it, in bullet point style, add key events you want to speak at or attend this year. Under each, define how it will add value to your growth.

Step 4. My Products

Put the 4th arrow from your name—"My Products." Under it, in a bullet point style, add key products you want to build this year. Under each, define the respective ROI.

Step 5. My Principles & Values

Put the 5th arrow from your name—"My Principles & Values." Under it, in a bullet point style, add all the principles and values you stand for. They will change, and it is normal. Your current year's goals shall align with your current principles and values.

Step 6. My Services

Put the 6th arrow from your name—"My Services." Under it, in bullet point style, add everything you can offer to the world aside from your main work. Your services shall aim to help others achieve their goals and become more successful. They may also serve as a side income.

Step 7. My Non-Negotiables

Put the 7th arrow from your name—"My Non-Negotiables." Under it, in a bullet point style, add everything dear to you [your family, friends, morning routine, any other routines, experiences you want to have, etc.], and under each, add the one essential action you must maintain to keep all of them in balance.

Step 8. My Do Not Dos
Put the 8th arrow from your name—"My Do Not Dos." Under it, in a bullet point style, add habits to stop, actions to change, reactions to reframe, and emotions to control, and then, under each, add the one essential action you must consistently execute to get the result you want.

Step 9. My New Habits
Put the 9th arrow from your name—"My New Habits." Under it, in a bullet point style, add new habits that will most certainly add value to your life and enhance your human value proposition [to your family, work/business, community], and then, under each, add the one essential action you must consistently execute to acquire them.

Step 10. My Meaningful Hobbies
Put the 10th arrow from your name—"My Meaningful Hobbies." Under it, in a bullet point style, add an activity or several activities that will help you grow as a person [not just a partner, a leader, an employee/colleague, a wife/husband, or mother/father] and then, under each, add the first three steps you need to take to get involved in this[these] activity[ies].

Step 11. My Giving Back

Put the 11th arrow from your name—"My Giving Back." Under it, in a bullet point style, add volunteering activities, pro bono mentoring, and free products you want to provide/release this year, and then, under each, add what you already have for each.

Step 12. My Investments

Put the 12th arrow from your name—"My Investments." Under it, in a bullet point style, add investments you can make throughout the year or need to make before the beginning of the following year to help you make 10X in any other Steps faster. These can include but shall not be limited to books, courses, gadgets, capital investments, coaching/mentoring, therapy, healthcare procedures or products, educational upgrades, etc.

What will work [better]

- If you draw your Life System by hand on a large sheet of white paper.
- If you don't share your Life System with your friends & family, co-workers, and team members.
- If you check and edit your Life System monthly [at the beginning or end of each month].
- If you leave enough space for the edits.
- If you look at your Life System as an experiment, not as a carved-in-stone must-do.
- If you apply curiosity and flexibility to your Life System.

- If you create your Life System with both short-term [1 year] and long-term [10 years] in mind.

APPENDIX 7

NEGOTIATION PREP WORKSHEET [NPW]

Negotiation Prep in 7 steps.

Step 1. Goal[s]
- What do I want to achieve [ideal outcome]?
- What am I ready to achieve [BATNA = best alternative to a negotiated agreement]?

Step 2. Strategy
- What is the best way to achieve my goal[s]?
- What negotiation style [analyst, accommodator, assertive] shall I start with, and how will I implement other styles throughout the negotiation?

Step 3. Issues
- What are my key concerns?
- What might be the key concerns of the other party?

Step 4. Positions
- Am I in a position of power in this negotiation?
- If not, what is my leverage?

- If yes, was I allowed to be in a position of power, or is it by my design?

Step 5. Interests
- What are my interests behind my goal[s]?
- What can be the interests of the other party? Why?

Step 6. Importance [not in terms of gain, but in terms of process]
- What is the most important for me in this negotiation [save face, help others save face, remain in the partnership, abort the partnership with mutual benefit, express my true intentions, share my deepest concerns, etc.]?
- What can be the most important thing for the other party?

Step 7. Benefit
- What do I have and am ready to give to get what I truly want?
- What does the other party have that is extremely important for me to get and not so important for them to keep?

APPENDIX 8

STARTUP HEATMAP WORKSHEET
[SHW]

Startup Heatmap in 7 heatpoints.

Heatpoint 1. Strategy

Assess your startup's vision, mission, and goals for clarity and alignment. Evaluate strategic initiatives, competitive positioning, and short- and long-term growth strategies.

Heatpoint 2. Product

Examine your product/service development, validation, and scalability. Assess market fit, user experience, feature prioritization, and product-market validation.

Heatpoint 3. Team

Evaluate your team's composition, dynamics, and effectiveness. Assess roles, responsibilities, communication channels, leadership dynamics, and team culture.

Heatpoint 4. Market

Gauge market traction and customer engagement. Analyze customer acquisition, retention rates, revenue growth, market share, and customer satisfaction.

Heatpoint 5. Operations

Optimize operational efficiency and resource allocation. Identify opportunities to streamline processes, improve workflows, and scale operations effectively.

Heatpoint 6. Capital

Evaluate funding strategies, financial health, and capital allocation. Assess fundraising efforts, cash flow management, profitability, and return on investment.

Heatpoint 7. Technology

Assess the technological infrastructure and capabilities of your startup. Evaluate scalability, security, innovation, and technological readiness to support current and future business objectives.

Heatpoints are what investors are looking for. Each heatpoint represents a strategic focus area. Startup Heatmap is a structured framework for assessing and prioritizing key areas within a startup in the most optimal sequence for fast growth. By breaking down the startup journey into specific heatpoints, you can effectively navigate the complexities of building and scaling your business while minimizing potential risks. Startup Heatmap is here to help you navigate critical heatpoints with clarity and confidence, enabling you to make informed decisions, allocate resources effectively, and drive sustainable growth and success.

APPENDIX 9

STARTUP PITCH PREP WORKSHEET [SPPW]

Startup Pitch Prep in 7 steps.

Step 1.

Did you know that [CUSTOMER CATEGORY] experience [PAIN, LACK, INEFFICIENCY]?

Step 2.

This is a [MARKET SIZE] X-dollar opportunity in [REGION] alone.

Step 3.

[PRODUCT NAME] is a [PRODUCT CATEGORY] designed to [VALUE PROPOSITION].

Step 4.

Unlike other alternatives, we, [KEY DIFFERENTIATOR].

Step 5.

The team includes [TEAM PROFILES], and we make money through [BUSINESS MODEL].

Step 6.

P 1. At our core, we are the [WELL-KNOWN ANALOGUE] for [ANALOGUE PRODUCT CATEGORY] *, and our vision is to [HOW WILL THE WORLD BE DIFFERENT? WHY DO YOU CARE?].

P 2. At our core, we help people to [ACTION] for [RESULT], and our vision is to [HOW WILL THE WORLD BE DIFFERENT? WHY DO YOU CARE?].

Step 7.

We have already executed [SIGNIFICANT MILESTONES], and you must be involved because [INVITE]!

* This part of Step 6 can be ignored if the association with any other product can harm your growth strategy. Instead, use part 2 of Step 6.

ABOUT THE AUTHOR

Alla Adam has been successfully future-proofing humans across the globe since 2003.

She is a publicly traded human on HumanIPO, an Affiliate Member of HeartMath Institute and Institute of Coaching at McLean Hospital, a Harvard Medical School, an Official Member of the Forbes Coaches Council, and an Advisory Council Member at Harvard Business Review.

She works with Fortune 500 companies and mentors startups at top accelerators and VC funds across six continents.

She has Executive Education certifications from Harvard Law School, Yale School of Management, and Kellogg School of Management.

Alla helps solve problems before they happen and pilots planes in between.

Made in the USA
Columbia, SC
22 June 2024